CAMBRIDGE LIBRARY COLLECTION

Books of enduring scholarly value

Polar Exploration

This series includes accounts, by eye-witnesses and contemporaries, of early expeditions to the Arctic and the Antarctic. Huge resources were invested in such endeavours, particularly the search for the North-West Passage, which, if successful, promised enormous strategic and commercial rewards. Cartographers and scientists travelled with many of the expeditions, and their work made important contributions to earth sciences, climatology, botany and zoology. They also brought back anthropological information about the indigenous peoples of the Arctic region and the southern fringes of the American continent. The series further includes dramatic and poignant accounts of the harsh realities of working in extreme conditions and utter isolation in bygone centuries.

The Career, Last Voyage, and Fate of Captain Sir John Franklin

The disappearance of Sir John Franklin's Arctic expedition of 1845 led to many rescue attempts, some by the British government, and some by private individuals. This short 1860 account of Franklin's life and of the search for him was written by the experienced naval officer Sherard Osborn (several of whose other works have been reissued in this series) with a view to inspiring the youth of Britain to follow the great explorer's example of duty and rectitude. Osborn (1822–75) had begun his naval career in the Far East, but was a pioneering commander of steam-powered ships, and his performance in the steam tender H.M.S. *Pioneer* in the 1850 rescue expedition confirmed the efficiency of this new technology in icy waters. Decorated for his role in the Crimean War, and later active in railway and telegraph technology, he continued to take an interest in Arctic exploration, and in steamships, until his death.

Cambridge University Press has long been a pioneer in the reissuing of out-of-print titles from its own backlist, producing digital reprints of books that are still sought after by scholars and students but could not be reprinted economically using traditional technology. The Cambridge Library Collection extends this activity to a wider range of books which are still of importance to researchers and professionals, either for the source material they contain, or as landmarks in the history of their academic discipline.

Drawing from the world-renowned collections in the Cambridge University Library and other partner libraries, and guided by the advice of experts in each subject area, Cambridge University Press is using state-of-the-art scanning machines in its own Printing House to capture the content of each book selected for inclusion. The files are processed to give a consistently clear, crisp image, and the books finished to the high quality standard for which the Press is recognised around the world. The latest print-on-demand technology ensures that the books will remain available indefinitely, and that orders for single or multiple copies can quickly be supplied.

The Cambridge Library Collection brings back to life books of enduring scholarly value (including out-of-copyright works originally issued by other publishers) across a wide range of disciplines in the humanities and social sciences and in science and technology.

The Career, Last Voyage,
and Fate of
Captain Sir John Franklin

Sherard Osborn

CAMBRIDGE
UNIVERSITY PRESS

University Printing House, Cambridge, CB2 8BS, United Kingdom

Cambridge University Press is part of the University of Cambridge.

It furthers the University's mission by disseminating knowledge in the pursuit of
education, learning and research at the highest international levels of excellence.

www.cambridge.org
Information on this title: www.cambridge.org/9781108071758

© in this compilation Cambridge University Press 2014

This edition first published 1860
This digitally printed version 2014

ISBN 978-1-108-07175-8 Paperback

This book reproduces the text of the original edition. The content and language reflect
the beliefs, practices and terminology of their time, and have not been updated.

Cambridge University Press wishes to make clear that the book, unless originally published
by Cambridge, is not being republished by, in association or collaboration with,
or with the endorsement or approval of, the original publisher or its successors in title.

THE CAREER LAST VOYAGE,

AND

FATE OF FRANKLIN.

FRANKLIN'S FIRST SIGHT OF THE SEA.

Frontispiece.

THE

CAREER, LAST VOYAGE, AND FATE

OF

CAPTAIN SIR JOHN FRANKLIN.

By CAPTAIN SHERARD OSBORN, C.B.

LONDON :

BRADBURY AND EVANS, 11, BOUVERIE STREET
1860.

The right of translation is reserved.

LONDON :
BRADBURY AND EVANS, PRINTERS, WHITEFRIARS.

PREFACE.

THERE cannot be a better, or a more noble career placed before the youth of England, and especially her sailors, as an ensample and encouragement, than that of the gallant, devoted officer whose services I have attempted to sketch in the following pages, some of which originally appeared in "Once a Week."

In all things, and under all circumstances, Franklin stands "sans peur et sans reproche:" he carved out his own high reputation by hard labour, zeal, and self-sacrifice, and was indebted neither to the interest of friends, nor to social position, for attaining the summit of naval fame.

Combining the highest qualities of hand and head, we find Franklin labouring equally well in the field of battle and in the field of maritime discovery ; and it is in the double character of naval hero and distinguished navigator, that he may be almost said to stand alone in our history.

SHERARD OSBORN,
CAPTAIN.

LONDON, *December*, 1859.

CONTENTS.

———•———

CHAPTERS I. II.

LIST OF ILLUSTRATIONS.

THE CAREER, LAST VOYAGE, AND FATE OF FRANKLIN.

CHAPTER I.

THE CAREER OF FRANKLIN.

"Themselves will fade, but not their memory,
And memory has the power to re-create them from the dust."
GOLDEN LEGEND.

A DAY of sunshine, and breeze waving the broad fields of golden wheat, and showing the bright blue of the corn-flower, and brilliant scarlet of the poppy, spreading for many an acre over the rich fat lands of Lincolnshire. Deep dykes, well marked by pollard and willow tree, wind far away in the distance, and tell how man had won these fens from the sea. A boy of well-knit, energetic frame, with black laughing eye, and dark ches-

nut curls, whose frank and broad English counte-
nance, lofty forehead, and well-formed chin are
indicative of future strength of character, may be
seen springing through those pleasant fields and
leaping the broad ditches, towards a wide and
sandy sea-shore, lashed by the foaming rollers of
the North Sea. Flushed with exertion, the perspi-
ration standing in big drops upon his white brow,
and his eye lit up with boyish enthusiasm, he
springs from the green turf to the sands, and hails
the big ocean with a shout of joy.

He had heard of it in his father's home at
Spilsby; he had read of it in the old grammar
school of Louth; he had been told how, upon that
ocean, the son of a country parson in an adjoining
county was humbling the pride of England's
enemy, and he now saw that great sea which was
to be his path to all the bright future of an earnest
imagination. It was all and more than his most
fervid hopes had pictured it. John Franklin
from that hour was a sailor.

Like Cooke, Dampier, and Nelson, his first essay

was on board a merchant-ship (into which he had been sent to disgust him of the sea), and like them the hardships of a sailor's life were more than counterbalanced in his opinion by the charms of its unceasing change, novelty, and excitement. All England was now in a fever of nautical enthusiasm, arising from the war with France. Nelson and the Nile! were the watchwords to stimulate British seamen to fresh naval triumphs, and young Franklin was just the lad to seek honour at the cannon's mouth. In those good old times, His Majesty George the Third, of glorious memory, rejoiced in ships named after personages tabooed in these more modern days, and on board of one entitled the Polyphemus, a stout sixty-four, commanded by, no doubt, an equally stout Captain Lawford, our young sailor (now fourteen years old) entered in 1800 as a quarter-deck petty officer, to make his first experiences of the Royal Navy.

Within a year, the Lincolnshire boy shared in the terrible sea-fight of Copenhagen, at the time when Nelson crushed the great Northern Confederacy formed for the humiliation of England; and, as leading ship in the attack, the Polyphemus covered herself with laurels, and young Franklin soon after returned home, to tell the old and young folks, in and around his home, of how the modern Dane had submitted to the sword of the descendant of their Viking forefathers. But John Franklin had intuitively learnt, that, for

"Sluggard's brow the laurel never grows ;
    Renown is not the child of indolent repose,"

and within two months he had succeeded in entering on board of the discovery ship Investigator, commanded by his relative Captain Flinders; this step, naturally, led his mind into those scientific pursuits which eventually rendered Franklin one of the most ardent and trustworthy of our geographical explorers.

For more than two years we see the Investigator —old, leaky, and crazy—such a vessel as, in our

day, would not be deemed fit even for the
work of a collier, struggling along the then unknown shores of that great southern continent to
which Flinders first gave the appropriate name of
Australia. It was a school of hardship and pain-
ful labour, yet not devoid of interest to the ardent
young sailor, and in all probability it was in making
there the first discoveries of many a mile of
coast, many a reef, many a haven, that Franklin's
mind became first imbued with that sincere love
of geographical exploration and maritime discovery, which subsequently formed so prominent a
feature in his future professional career.

Flinders was exactly the man to awaken such
feelings in one so intelligent as young Franklin.
He was one of that goodly company of circum-
navigators who had won for England the honour
of having really explored the great South Sea.
He could tell of Otaheite, and explain how our
rough uncared-for seamen of that day, forsook their
country and king for the love of its warm-hearted
people ; he had witnessed the ferocity of the Sand-

wich Islanders, and could thrill his listeners with
that awful hour of murder, and cannibalism, in
which the greatest of England's navigators fell.
He had weathered many a danger upon the inhospitable shores of the then unknown Australia,
and often navigated in high southern latitudes.
He had in a little boat in bygone days circumna-
vigated the tempestuous coasts of Van Diemen's
Land, and shared with Bass the honour of discovering the strait which bears the name of the
latter. Clever, modest, and unassuming, Flinders
formed the character, and imparted much of his
knowledge and information to the youth, whose
destiny it was, in after years, to fall as the discoverer
of the North-West Passage.

Napoleon the First was then, with characteristic
ambition and far-sightedness, striving to establish a
lien by priority of discovery, upon the coast of the
great continent with which Cooke's voyages had
only made Europe partially acquainted. Flinders
and his gallant little band of associates succeeded,
however, in forestalling the French navigators in

THE WRECK OF THE PORPOISE.

every quarter, exhibiting a rare degree of perseverance, zeal, and ability, for which he has not in Great Britain ever received due credit. At last the glorious old Investigator showed unmistakeable signs of being no longer seaworthy, and her crew were likewise nigh worn out with scurvy and dysentery. She was condemned at Port Jackson, and Franklin embarked in 1803, with his captain and shipmates, on board H.M.S. Porpoise, for a passage to England.

Passing north-about round Australia, the Porpoise with two consorts found themselves entangled amongst the reefs, then but little known, of Torres Straits. Under treble-reefed topsails they seek their way; in the darkness of the night of August 18th, the leading ship descries breakers close ahead, and as she falls upon the reef, fires a gun to warn the vessels in her wake. The Porpoise in a few minutes was staved and dismasted, but happily she fell over with her deck towards the reef, and her bottom thus saved her from total destruction in the charging rollers of the South Sea. One of their

consorts struck, and, less fortunate than the Porpoise, fell towards the sea, and broke up so as to
occasion considerable loss of life ; the other vessel
fled in a dastardly manner, and her commander
only escaped the punishment due to such an offence,
by himself and the vessel he commanded foundering
in the Indian Ocean. Our young sailor now found
himself one of ninety-four souls on a sand-bank—
very little more than a wash, and 400 feet long:
with the then inhospitable coast of Australia 180
miles distant. The nearest point at which succour
was to be found was Port Jackson, 750 miles
off; thither Flinders proceeded in an open boat,
and by God's mercy reached it, in time to return
with the means of rescuing all his officers and
crew.

An opportunity offering for China, Franklin
and some of his companions proceeded thither, under
command of Lieut. Fowler, with the object of
returning home in one of the Honourable Company's ships.

On the last day of January, 1804, a magnificent

fleet of fifteen East Indiamen are putting to sea, from the Canton River. Franklin has obtained a passage in the Earl Camden, commanded by stout-hearted Nathaniel Dance, the commodore of this fleet, which is laden with millions' worth of Chinese products. Most of the ships are painted as if they were line-of-battle ships, and though not fitted as men-of-war, the good traders of Leaden-hall had provided guns and men sufficient to prevent their argosies falling without resistance into the hands of privateering Frenchmen. The 14th February finds them nearing Pulo Auor, one of the last islands seen before shaping a course for the Straits of Malacca; the China fleet are well in hand. Strange sails are seen, and soon ascertained to be the then notorious Marengo, 74, Admiral Linois, and his three satellite frigates. The Gallic chief knows it is the long-sought prize, the China fleet, and hastens towards it, but is surprised to find fifteen ships in order of battle, some of them more warlike-looking than others, but all ready to fight. He heaves to, in the hope that during the night the

merchantmen of England will flee, but daylight
of the 15th finds them all as they had passed the
night, at their quarters, guns shotted, and more
prepared to do battle for the red flag which waved
defiantly from their mizen peaks, than on the
previous day. Linois, more than ever puzzled,
does not attack, until the English bear away under
easy sail; he then essays to cut off the rearmost
ships. He counts without his host; the gallant
Dance throws out the signal, "Tack! bear
down, and engage the enemy!" A shout of joy
went through that noble fleet of merchant sailors,
and to the astonishment of the Frenchman, he had
the whole swarm about his ears. He made all
sail away; Dance, in the Earl Camden, directed a
general chase, and then was seen a sight, of which
every Englishman should cherish the recollection,
—of a French squadron of men-of-war, perfectly
equipped, led by one of their most distinguished
officers, retreating before a fleet of armed merchant
ships; and well might Franklin be proud in after
years of having thus shared, as a middy, in the

honours of Dance's victory. Before another year had passed over his head, he was signal midshipman on board the Bellerophon, 74, and on the memorable 21st Oct. 1805, he fought again with Nelson, at Trafalgar. We see the Lincolnshire boy pass through all the phases from childhood to manhood, from the sky-larking middy to the steady trustworthy lieutenant—tempered in a school of patient perseverance, and not spoilt by constant success ; he saw the failure at Flushing ; he marked how the under-estimating of a foe brought down upon his profession the mischances of the American War ; and in the disastrous attempt to capture New Orleans he was for the first time wounded.

At last in 1814, came peace—a long peace—after a long war, a stark calm after a terrible tempest, which left all Europe desolate. The passions, feelings, and energies which so long a period of excitement and danger had called into action, especially in such a service as the triumphant navy of England, had now to find vent in other channels. Thousands were thrown out of employ-

ment, sailors died of starvation, hundreds of officers
laboured, on a wretched pittance, to show they deserved a better fate than to starve as half-pay lieu-
tenants.   Some went to our colonies, others sought
service under foreign states; Australia, Canada,
Africa, and even the present independent states of
South America, owe much to these restless enterprising spirits.   Franklin turned again to his early
love, Maritime Discovery, for which the training he
had undergone under the distinguished Flinders
now stood him in good stead.

The young, enthusiastic, intelligent lieutenant,
then thirty-one years of age, was just the man to win
the kind offices of keen observers of merit like Sir
Joseph Banks and Sir John Barrow.   The long
vexed question of a passage to the Pacific through
the Arctic zone was just revived.   The writings of
Scoresby, an observant and skilful fisher of whales,
attracted public attention to Arctic discovery;
scientific men adopted and enlarged upon his
views; and at last, after long years of trial and
disappointment, England achieved, as we will here-

after relate, the problem she undertook to solve —the discovery of the North West Passage to the Indies—by that same Franklin who may now be said to represent the Alpha and Omega of modern Arctic exploration.

CHAPTER II.

———•———

" Rise up, and look from where thou art,
 And scatter with unselfish hands
 Thy freshness on the barren sands
 And solitudes of death."

LONGFELLOW.

On the 25th of April, 1818, the first Arctic
expedition of this century was sailing down the
Thames. The discovery brigs were the Dorothea
and Trent; Capt. Buchan commanded the former,
Lieut. John Franklin the latter. They were bound
to the Pacific Ocean by way of the North Pole!
The Admiralty had especially enjoined the gallant
leader to pass between Spitzbergen and Greenland,
and before "leaving England to fix with Captain
John Ross (who was going by way of Baffin's Bay)
a rendezvous in the Pacific Ocean!"

We must not smile at what has been subsequently proved to be the unfounded confidence

of success arising from utter ignorance of the task to be accomplished; but try to picture to ourselves how difficult it then was, for a nation, an Admiralty, and a navy that had conquered all else upon the high seas, to believe that mere ice was going to stay their march of triumph through the frigid zone.

Assuredly none on board the stout, but ugly little brigs thought so. There was a supreme ignorance of Arctic navigation in those days, beyond perhaps the notion that some hard knocks might be expected, to guard against which, as much wood and iron as could be well added to the original hulls of the Trent and Dorothea were bolted on them in a certain dock in Shadwell. To be sure some had pointed to the Hon. Captain Phipps' essay in 1793, and shook their heads at an attempt to cross the Pole; but the sanguine smiled at their fears, and spoke of those old days as only a better reason for a fresh attempt. Oh! those were days when British fleets could not relieve Gibraltar from blockade; when sailors worked for the

weather-gauge, fought by Shrewsbury clock, and
hauled off to repair damages ; when Rodney had to
hang Captains, and Tory ships engaged an enemy
whilst Whig ships held their wind! Times had
changed since then. The Nile, Copenhagen, and
Trafalgar had altered our naval tone, and made all
things possible. Franklin felt as confident, on that
25th April, of reaching the Pacific as that there was
his pendant fluttering from the truck of the Trent;
and it was impossible to look at that bright eye
lit up with enthusiasm, without feeling a kindred
certainty of success. None thought of danger, all
looked at the goal,—the Pacific. The storms, the
ice, the iron-bound shores of Greenland and Spitzbergen were forgotten ; all talked of the blue skies
of the ocean with the gentle name, and of the
orange groves of fair Otaheite. The Norse-kings of
old ne'er sailed with stouter hearts for the North,
or raised braver shouts of Skoal! to the North-land
Skoal! than did our bold countrymen on that fair
April morn.

*   *   *   *

Six months afterwards (Oct. 22), two weather-beaten brigs arrived from the North Sea ; they were the Dorothea and Trent again—the former so shattered as to be no longer sea-worthy, the latter almost as much damaged. Their tale was a wondrous one, men heard it with bated breath, and women thanked their God that such bold seamen had been spared.

Within a month after they left Greenwich, the vessels found themselves in a polar sea, strewn with ice-fields, and darkened with fogs, alternating with sudden storms. Franklin's vessel was discovered to be so leaky from some shipwright's carelessness, that half a watch of men were ever at the pumps ! They wind on, however, and seek their way to the North until the grim mountains of Spitzbergen, clad in everlasting ice, rise above the horizon. Heavy snow-storms come on with a bitter tempe-rature ; " *tons weight* " of frozen snow-flakes, agglutinated by the freezing sea-spray, cover the ships alow and aloft; the brigs are mere icebergs under sail; the very ropes become as thickly clad

c

as pine branches in a Siberian forest. The
astonished but light-hearted crews laugh at the
sight, while constantly removing with axes and
shovels, the masses of ice and snow which encum-
ber their vessels, and endanger the spars. Unable
to proceed beyond Spitzbergen, they seek a
harbour, and thence issue twice again to battle
with the polar-ice. The vessels return to Magda-
lena Bay, each time more shattered from the
unequal conflict. On the last occasion God's
Providence and mercy alone saved all from total
shipwreck and an awful death. The brigs are
caught in a furious storm, and compelled to heave
to under storm stay-sails. Next morning (June
30), the ice is seen along the lee, with a terrible
sea beating upon it—a hopeless lee-shore indeed!
Close-reefed sails are set in the hope of clearing
the danger. Vain hope! in such a sea, with such
dull sailing craft! Franklin, in the Trent, sees
that Buchan, who was to leeward of him, cannot
weather it, and that the Dorothea is about to take
the desperate step of "taking the pack," a step

resorted to only as a "dernier ressort," in pre-
ference to falling, broadside on, into such a frightful
scene of breakers and broken ice. God help them!
was the involuntary cry of those on board the
Trent, and the words were the more earnest that
all felt the same fate would soon be their own.
The Dorothea wore, and dashed before sea and
wind towards what looked certain destruction;
those in the Trent held their breath as they
watched the daring exploit; the suspense lasted a
moment only, for the vessel, like a snow-flake
before the storm, was swept into the hideous scene
of foam, spray, and tumbling fragments, which
formed a wall impenetrable to mortal eye-sight.
Whether lost or saved, those on board the Trent
would never know until they likewise were forced
to take a step which seemed like rushing into the
portals of certain death. Every hour convinced
Franklin that such a measure was inevitable, and
when he had made all ready, he gave, in decisive
tones, the order to "put up the helm!"

"No language," says a powerful writer and eye-witness, "can convey an adequate idea of the terrific grandeur of the effects produced by the collision of the ice and the tempestuous ocean," or " of the great calmness and resolution of all our crew." As they near the frightful scene, Franklin glances quickly for one opening more promising than another. There is none; it is one immense line of frightful breakers, immense blocks of ice heaving, rearing, and crashing against one another with a roar above which the loud voice of the gallant leader can hardly be heard. On the crest of a huge wave the little Trent dashes herself into the scene of turmoil ;—there is a frightful shock, the crew are flung upon the deck, and the masts bend like willow wands. "Hold on! for your lives, and stand to the helm, lads !" shouts the clear bold voice of him who had already faced death in many forms. "Aye, aye! sir," is the cheery response from many a pale face but firm-set mouth. A roller dashes itself against the stern of the brig ; she must be engulphed, or be forced ahead—God be praised ! the gallant Trent forges ahead, with a weak and staggering gait, every timber cracking, and the ship's bell tolling mournfully as if it were her requiem. Now, thrown broadside on, the floe-pieces threaten to beat in her side, then, tossed by the sea over ice-block after ice-block, it seemed indeed as if every minute would be her last. For some hours this trial of strength and fortitude endured—then the storm passed away, as speedily as it had set in; and apart from gratitude at their own providential escape, they joyed to see in the distance the poor Dorothea still afloat and her crew in safety.

With broken timbers, sprung beams, and the Dorothea's larboard side forced in, both vessels exhibiting internally the fearful effects of the external shocks to which they had been subjected, the shattered expedition returned to Spitzbergen. Franklin still urged that he might be allowed to proceed alone, whilst Buchan returned home with the Dorothea for repairs. Buchan, as senior officer, wisely ruled otherwise, and the two vessels returned, as we have already told.

Within a year, we again find Lieutenant John Franklin returning to the frigid zone; but this time for boat exploration of the coasts of Arctic America, to be reached overland.   In 1819 he left England, accompanied by Dr. the present Sir John Richardson, George Back, * and Robert Hood, midshipmen, and John Hepburn, an English seaman.   They were heard of at long and uncertain intervals; and eventually, in 1822, all but poor Robert Hood returned to astonish their countrymen with the tale of their hardships, fortitude, and honourable achievements. The tale of Franklin's journey fully bears out the glowing eulogium of Sir John Barrow: "It adds," says Sir John, "another to the many splendid records of enterprise, zeal, and energy of our seamen: of that cool and intrepid conduct which never forsakes them on occasions the most trying— that unshaken constancy and perseverance in situations the most arduous, the most distressing, and sometimes the most hopeless, that can befall human beings; and it furnishes a beautiful example of the

* The present Admiral Sir George Back.

triumph of mental and moral energy over mere brute strength, in the simple fact, that out of fifteen individuals inured from their birth to cold, fatigue, and hunger, no less than ten (native landsmen), were so subdued by the aggravation of those evils to which they had been habituated, as to give themselves up to indifference, insubordination, and despair, and finally to sink down and die; whilst of five British seamen, unaccustomed to the severity of the climate, and the hardships attending it, one only fell, and that one by the hands of an assassin. A light buoyant heart, a confidence in their own powers, supported by a firm reliance on a merciful Providence, never once forsook them, and brought them through such misery and distress as rarely, if ever, have been surmounted."

It is indeed a tale (I speak of Franklin's narrative) which should be put into the hands of those youths of England who desire to emulate the deeds and fame of such men as himself and his followers. It is an Iliad in prose, and replete with pictures of rare devotion to the most ennobling of causes, the advancement of human knowledge. A generous and chivalrous spirit breathes through every page, and sheds a lustre not only on every act of the leader, but likewise of those who were his comrades and friends in many a sad hour of need and danger. Those terrible marches; the laborious exploration of the regions around the mouths of the Mackenzie and Coppermine Rivers; the long, bitter starvation of the winter; the murder of Hood; the destruction of the assassin and the cannibal; the intrepid effort of Richardson to swim across the freezing Coppermine to save his comrades; Back's fearful winter journey to bring succour to his chief; are all tales which should be household words by every English fire-side.

Franklin's safe return to England excited the most enthusiastic public interest : his devotion and gallantry stamped him as no ordinary man in the estimation of his countrymen, and the Admiralty, having during his absence made him a Commander, now promoted him to the rank of Captain.

Thus, in twenty-two years, Franklin had

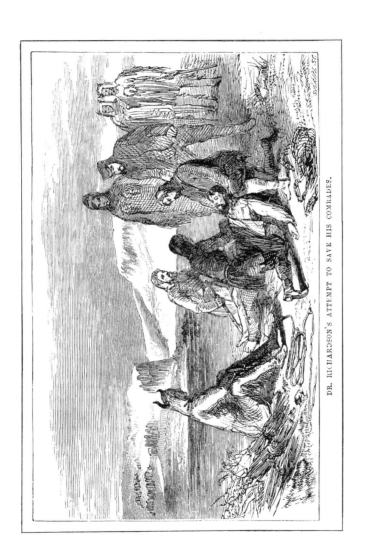

DR. RICHARDSON'S ATTEMPT TO SAVE HIS COMRADES.

achieved all that it was possible for energy and ability to win as a sailor. He had won fame and a captain's commission ; henceforward the rules of the Royal Navy compelled him, as it has many other able men, to be content with the dull level of a seniority promotion to the rank of admiral. Yet Franklin was not disheartened ; zeal for his country's fame, more than his own advancement, was the great secret of his professional success, and he longed again to be up and doing.

It was in 1823 that he married his first wife, Eleanor Porden. She seems largely to have partaken of the enterprising spirit of her husband, and when, within two short years (1825), Franklin stood by her side and held in his hand the summons of his country to proceed upon another Arctic expedition, and with his heart overflowing with sorrow and pride, told her how sad the conflict between love for her, and duty to his country and profession, noble Eleanor Porden thought not of self, though she knew the hand of death was already pressing her down to

the land of long rest and silence, and that no more
in this world would she meet her beloved husband.
Forgetting self, she urged him bravely on to the
fulfilment of the task his God and country had
assigned him; and, with her weak and faltering
hands, worked a flag which he was to spread to the
winds, and think of her at the moment when she
proudly hoped he would reach the polar sea, that
great step towards the North-West Passage—the
guerdon for which England's naval chivalry then
longed, and which this noble woman felt assured
her beloved husband must one day win.

Thus, in this prosaic age, went forth again Captain John Franklin, in true knightly mood to
endure, labour, and accomplish much, but
without achieving the darling object of his
heart. He and his worthy, steadfast friend and
companion, Sir John Richardson, in open boats,
with much peril and suffering, laid down, however,
sufficient of the coast of Arctic America to assure
all geographers that along that shore would one
day be discovered the long-sought passage to the

Indies; and in 1827 they returned to receive again at the hands of their admiring countrymen, all the honours that could be bestowed, and that they so well deserved.

Three years after the death of his first wife Eleanor, Franklin married Jane Griffin, and it is singular to observe how well Franklin placed his affections upon two women who, each in their sphere of action, stand forth as charming instances of the British matron. Eleanor Franklin dying, knowing that she never more may see the man she loves, urges him on to the execution of his duty, and enables Franklin to lay down, by his discoveries in Arctic America, the foundation upon which he is hereafter to erect his own title to immortality in this world,—and Jane Franklin, better known as Lady Franklin, seventeen years subsequently, not only supports her heroic husband in the great wish of his gallant heart, but when, by God's decree, the secret of his success was hidden from mortal ken, owing to the self-sacrifice of those martyrs to science, she, the wife worthy of such a naval hero, steadfastly, earnestly laboured for eleven long years, sacrificing health and patrimony to learn the history of her husband's fate; and, in spite of many failures, many disappointments, official rebuffs and private hostility, though not without much sympathy, at last God be thanked, worked out the great object of her woman's faith and love—That he indeed, John Franklin, had not lived, laboured, or died in vain.

CHAPTER III.

THE LAST VOYAGE OF FRANKLIN.

———◆———

" And there they lay till all their bones were bleach'd
And lichen'd into colour with the crags."
TENNYSON.

" THERE is yet one thing left undone, whereby
a great mind may become notable," wrote worthy
Master Purchas :—that one deed was the discovery
of a North-West Passage to the Indies. Many
long years afterwards, the words of the good Dean
of St. Paul's sounded like a trumpet-call to his
countrymen, and many an aspiring spirit essayed to
do that deed whereby bright honour and immortality were to be won. The veil which hid from
human ken the mysteries of the Arctic zone, was
not to be rent by one bold stroke ; it was to be the
test of British perseverance, patience, and hardihood. The frozen north would only reveal its

wonders slowly and unwillingly to the brave men who devoted themselves to the task. The dread realms of frost and silence were only to be penetrated by the labours of two generations of seamen and travellers. The consummation of the discovery of the North-West Passage was to be obtained but by the self-sacrifice of a hundred heroes.

From 1815 to 1833 England sent forth her sons to the north in repeated expeditions by sea and land. The earnestness of many eminent public men, members of the Royal Society—such as Sir John Barrow and Sir Francis Beaufort—kept general interest directed to those regions in which Frobisher, Baffin, Davis, and Fox had so nobly ventured. There were no falterers; every call for volunteers was nobly responded to by officers of the Royal Navy; and John Franklin, Richardson, John and James Ross, Parry, Back, and King, with much devotion, toil, and suffering, forced open the portals beyond which the Elizabethan school of discoverers had not been able to penetrate, and added much to our knowledge of the

geography and physical condition of the Arctic zone
between Greenland and Behring's Straits. Fifteen
years of labour had failed, however, to solve the

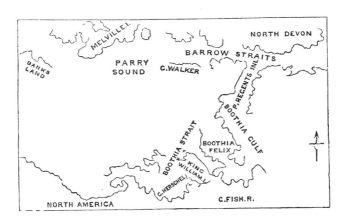

question as to the actual existence of a water
communication between the Pacific and Atlantic.
Repeated disappointment had damped public zeal.
Just at this juncture, between 1838 and 1843, the
success of Captain Sir James Ross in an expedition
to the Antarctic Pole with H.M.S. Erebus and
Terror, as well as the completion of the northern
coast-line of America by the Hudson Bay Com-

pany's servants, Dease and Simpson, caused the attention of the nation to again revert to its old channel—the North-West Passage.   Anno Domini 1844 found England with a surplus revenue, a vast body of naval officers begging for employment, and eager for any opportunity of winning honours and distinction; and H.M.S. Erebus and Terror, safe and sound from the perils of Antarctic seas, riding at anchor off Woolwich.   All was most propitious for carrying out the darling object of the then venerable Secretary of the Admiralty.   A mind like that of Sir John Barrow's, richly stored with the records of his country's glories in the exploration of every quarter of the globe, was keenly alive to the importance of keeping her still in the vanguard of geographical discovery : and it must be remembered that he had lived in a century when men, in spite of a long and terrible war, were almost yearly excited by the world-wide fame of the discoveries of Anson, Cooke, Flinders, and Mungo Park.   Was it not natural, therefore, that he, and such as he, should desire to add to those triumphs the achievement of the greatest geographical problem man ever undertook to solve.

The chart of the Arctic regions was in the unsatisfactory condition shown in the chart on the preceding page.

How simple an undertaking it appeared, to connect the water in which Parry had sailed to Melville Island, in 1819, with Dease and Simpson's easternmost position off the coast of America in 1838.

The summer of 1844 saw many an eager face poring over that Arctic chart. Whisperings were heard that Sir John Barrow, Beaufort, Parry, Sabine, Ross, and Franklin himself, had expressed strong opinions in favour of another effort. The Royal Society, through its president, the Marquis of Northampton, was known to have urged the resumption of Arctic exploration upon the Government and Admiralty. Many an enthusiastic officer strove hard, by zeal and interest, to insure being one of those selected for the glorious work. Then it was that Fitzjames, and such men as Graham

Gore, Fairholme, Hodgson, and Des Vœux, succeeded in enrolling themselves on the list of the
chosen few who were next year to sail for the far
north-west.   We see them now, as they told us so,
and with glistening eye prophesied their own success.   Gallant hearts ! they now sleep amidst the
scenes of their sore trial, but triumphant discovery.

It was at one time intended that Fitzjames
(whose genius and energy marked him as no ordinary officer) should command the expedition ; but
just at this time Sir John Franklin was heard to
say that he considered the post to be his birthright
as the senior Arctic explorer in England.   He had
recently returned from his post as Governor of Van
Diemen's Land : his sensitive and generous spirit
chafed under the unmerited treatment he had experienced from the then Secretary of State for the
Colonies, and, sick of civil employment, he naturally
turned again to his profession, as a better field for
the ability and devotion he had wasted on a thank-
less office.   Sanguine of success, forgetful of past
suffering, he claimed his right to command the

latest, as he had led the earliest, of modern Arctic expeditions.

Directly it was known that he would go if asked, the Admiralty were of course only too glad to avail themselves of the experience of such a man; but Lord Haddington, then First Lord, with that kindness which ever distinguished him, suggested that Franklin might well rest at home on his laurels. " I might find a good excuse for not letting you go, Sir John," said the peer, " in the tell-tale record which informs me that you are sixty years of age." " No, no, my lord," was Franklin's rejoinder, " I am only *fifty-nine !* " Before such earnestness all scruples yielded—the offer was officially made and accepted—to Sir John Franklin was confided the Arctic Expedition, consisting of H.M.S. Erebus, in which he hoisted his pendant, and H.M.S. Terror, commanded by Captain Crozier, who had recently accompanied Sir James Ross in his wonderful voyage to the Antarctic seas.

The 18th of May, 1845, found the Erebus and Terror at Greenhithe in the Thames. On board of

each ship there were sixty-nine officers and men;
every possible corner was carefully filled with
stores and provisions—enough, they said, for three
years; and, for the first time in Arctic annals, these
discovery vessels each had auxiliary screws and
engines of twenty-horse power.   Hope rode high in
every breast, and the cry of Hurrah! for Behring's
Straits! succeeded their last hearty cheer as the
gallant ships weighed on the morrow for Baffin's Bay.

A month they sailed across the Atlantic before
they reached their first halting-place, Disco, or the
Whale Fish Islands, on the west coast of Greenland, in latitude 69° north.   Thither a store-ship
had accompanied them from England, in order that
the expedition might be completed with every
necessary up to the latest moment before entering
the polar ice.   That voyage of thirty days had
served to make the officers and men thoroughly
acquainted with their chief, and with each other.
Of him, the warm-hearted Fitzjames writes: "That
Sir John was delightful; that all had become very
fond of him, and that he appeared remarkable for

energetic decision in an emergency. The officers were remarkable for good feeling, good humour and great talents; whilst the men were fine hearty sailors, mostly from the northern sea-ports." Love already, it is apparent, as much as duty, bound together the gallant hearts on board the Erebus and Terror.

Away from Disco they sped with all haste; the Bay of Baffin is fairly entered, and their long and arduous labours commence with an Arctic tempest so severe, that their brother seamen of the store-ship, hastening homeward, thought with anxiety of the deep-laden Erebus and Terror. He who is strong to save guides the gallant barks, however, past the dangers of an iron-bound coast, and amongst the huge, ghost-like ice-bergs which glimmer through the storm. We see them, in better weather, urging under all sail, their strong but clumsy ships, before a favourable gale, along that coast of Greenland, every headland of which has its record of human trial, and noble endurance. There, the lofty headland of Sanderson-his-Hope (of a North-west Passage) rears its crest of black

granite, rich with crimson lichen, and crowned
with snow. Norseman, and Dane, and Englishman, have alike sailed under its stupendous cliffs,
or sought shelter in quaint Uppernavik which
nestles at its feet. The Erebus and Terror may
not delay. Greenland has no charms for men
whose leader already talks sanguinely of the yet
far distant Mackenzie and Copper-mine rivers.

The floes and broad masses of the Middle-ice now
rise upon their sight; the northern horizon gleams
with reflected light from the frozen surface of the
sea; the south wind fails; the ships sail from the
black mists and fog-laden atmosphere common to
open water in the Arctic regions, into the bright skies,
smooth lanes, and mirror-like pools generally found
amongst the pack during the summer season.
The ice is streaming southward; the eager novices
in either ship, look forward with delight to the
first onset with the foe they have come to do battle
with. Wiser heads know, that mother-wit will
do more than dashing gallantry, in the conflict
with packed ice; the sails are taken in so as to

reduce the speed, and the experienced ice-master
from the crow's nest at the mast-head selects the
weakest looking point through which to force the
ships into a lane of water, that winds snake-like
along the landward edge of the pack.

"So-ho! steady—steer her with a small helm,
my lad!" bawls out, in strong North-country
dialect, the honest old ice-pilot, who has grown
grey killing whales in Greenland. "Stand by to
brail up the after-sails, if you please, sir; and to
pack all the canvas upon her directly we break
through the pack edge," he urges to the officer of
the watch. The churning, and growling of the
ice now strikes upon the ear, and at the same
moment the Erebus and Terror take it manfully.
There is a shock: for a second the pieces of ice
hold their ground, but they yield to the weight of
the ships; one mass tilts up, and slips over
another, another sinks under the bows, and is
heard scraping along the bottom of the ship; the
road is opening. "Hard up with the helm,"
shouts the ice-master, and at the same time the

sail is set forward to urge the ship faster through the pack; the speed accelerates, and in a few minutes they are fairly in the ice. We need not follow them in their daily labour. Ice is now on every hand: open water scarce. The crews often drag the ships for hours with ropes, along the edge of the land-floe, that is still fast to the face of the glacier which curves round Melville Bay. Now we see them perfectly beset, the vessels secured to the lowest icebergs that can be found: they studiously avoid those lofty masses which, with spires, and domes, and steeples, resemble huge cathedrals of crystal,—for they know that such icebergs are prone to turn over, or break up suddenly, and would infallibly crush any ship that might be near them.

For a while the discovery ships meet the whaling-vessels of Aberdeen and Hull, striving, like themselves, to get through the loose ice into the waters of Pond's Bay. On July 26th they part company from the last of them, and pursue their solitary course alone. Again they pass from

the northern edge of the pack into open water,—
if such may be called an open sea, where icebergs
are strewn plentifully. The course is now shaped for
Lancaster Sound. August has set in; the sun, which
has hitherto wheeled round the heavens without
setting, again commences to dip below the horizon;
its absence and already declining power is marked
by the nightly formation of thin, glass-like ice,
known as bay-ice.   The south wind freshens; the
Erebus and Terror press on, staggering in a heavy
sea, all the more remarkable that a hundred miles
of ice have just been passed through behind them.
The great entrance of Lancaster-his-Sound breaks
out of the clouds to the westward.   Capes War-
render, and Hay, frown grimly over the angry sea,
backed by lofty mountain ranges, whose dark precipices, streaked with snow, look as if they were
formed of steel, and inlaid with silver.

"On, on! to the westward!" is the cry.   Why
need to stop and erect cairns, and deposit records
of their progress!   Do they not intend to pass into
the Pacific next year?   Have not they ordered

their letters to be directed to Petropaulskoi and the
Sandwich Isles! Why lose one precious hour at
the threshold of their labour?

The ice is again seen: it extends along the
southern side of Barrow's Straits, and is streaming
out into Baffin's Bay. The ships haul in for the
coast of North Devon. The scene changes con-
siderably from what our explorers have seen in
Greenland. No glaciers stretch from the interior,
and launch their long, projecting tongues into the
sea: no icy cliffs reflect there the colours of the
emerald and turquoise: Arctic vegetation, wretched
as it is, does not gladden the eyesight in even the
most favoured spots. They have passed from a
region of primary rock into one of magnesian limestone. Greenland is a paradise, in an Arctic point of
view, to the land they have now reached: it is desolation's abiding-place; yet not deficient in the pictu-
resque. The tall and escarped cliffs are cut by action
of frost and thaws into buttresses and abutments,
which, combined with broken castellated summits,
give a Gothic-like aspect to the shores of North

STOPPED BY THE ICE.

Devon. Valleys and plains are passed, all of one uniform dun colour; they consist simply of barren limestone. The sterility of the land is, however, somewhat compensated for, by the plentiful abundance of animal life upon the water. The seal, the whale, and the walrus are there; whilst wild fowl in large flocks feed in the calm spots under beetling cliffs, or in shallow lakes, which can be looked down upon from the mast-head.

It is not far to the entrance of Wellington Channel; they reach Beechey Island, and mark the value of the bay within it as a wintering-place, and its central position with respect to the channels leading towards Cape Walker, Melville Island, or Regent's Inlet. Ice again impedes their progress. Their first instructions from the Admiralty were to try to the south-west from Cape Walker. They cannot now advance in that direction, for it is a hopeless block of heavy floes; but Wellington Channel is open, and smiles and sparkles in blue and sunlit waves, as if luring them to the north-west. Why not try a north-about passage round

the Parry Islands ? urges Fitzjames. Franklin
agrees with him that anything is better than
delay, and at any rate they determine to explore
it, and ascertain whither it led. Away they press
northward, until what is now known as Grinnell
Land rises a-head, and they have to turn more to
the west. From Wellington Channel they pass
between Baillie Hamilton Island and the striking
cliffs of Cape Majendie into Penny's Strait.

Eager eyes are straining from the mast-head ; is
it a mere bay, or is it a channel they are sailing
through ? " Water, water !—large water ! " replies
the ice-master from his eyry to the anxious queries
of the veteran leader. Away, away they press !—
every studding sail alow, and aloft. The old ships
never went so fast before—no, not on that great
day in their history when they were the first to
sail along the Victoria continent of the Southern
Pole. From 74½° to 77° north latitude they pushed
up this noble strait ; but not, as they hoped, to
reach an open or navigable sea, but to find as we
found in 1852—a wide expanse of water much

choked up with ice, extending from the head of Wellington Channel far to the westward for hundreds of miles. Baffled, but not beaten, the prows of the stout ships are again turned southward, and, aided by a greater share of success than has fallen to the lot of those who have come after Sir John Franklin in those same quarters, the gallant Erebus and Terror sailed down a channel which is thus proved to exist between Cornwallis and Bathurst Islands, and entered Barrow's Straits at a point nearly due north of Cape Walker, in which direction Franklin was now constrained to alone look for a route whereby to reach the sea off the coast of North America.

It was well known that this southern course was that of his predilection; founded on his judgment and experience. There are many in England who can recollect him pointing on his chart to the western entrance of Simpson's Strait and the adjoining coast of North America, and saying :—

"If I can but get down there, my work is done; thence it's all plain sailing to the westward."

Franklin might well say this, since he and Richardson had explored nearly all that coast of Arctic America towards Behring's Straits.

The fortnight, however, which had been spent in Wellington Channel, was the short period of navigation common to the ice-choked seas within Lancaster Sound. September and an Arctic autumn broke upon them. Who that has navigated those seas can ever forget the excitement and danger of the autumn struggle with ice, snow-storm, and lee-shores. We see those lonely barks in the heart of a region which appears only to have been intended to test man's enterprise, and to show him that, after all, he is but a poor weak creature. Channels surround them in all directions, down and up which, let the wind blow from any quarter, an avalanche of broken floes and ugly packed ice rolls down, and threatens to engulph all that impedes its way, checked alone by the isles which strew Barrow's Straits and serve, like the teeth of a harrow, to rip up and destroy the vast ice-fields which are launched against them. Around each

island, as well as along the adjacent coasts, and
especially at projecting capes and headlands,
mountains of floe-pieces are piled mass on top of
mass, as if the frozen sea would invade the frozen
land. The Erebus and Terror, under the skilful
hands of their noble ships' companies, flit to and
fro ; seek shelter first under one point and then
another. Franklin, Crozier, and Fitzjames are
battling to get into Peel Channel, between Capes
Walker and Bunny. The nights are becoming
rapidly longer, the temperature often falls fifteen
degrees below freezing point, the pools of water on
the great ice-fields as well as on the land are again
firmly frozen over. The wild fowl and their off-
spring are seen hastening south ; the plumage of
the ptarmigan and willow grouse is already plentifully sprinkled with white ; the mountain-tops
and ravines are loaded with snow, which will
not melt away for twelve long months. Enough
has been done to satisfy Franklin that a further
advance this season will be impossible. Winter
quarters must be sought ; there is none nearer that

they know of than Beechey Island; the Erebus
and Terror bear away for it. Fortune favours
them, that they are not caught in the fatal grip of
the winter-pack, and drifted out into the Atlantic,
as many subsequent voyagers have been. Their
haven is reached, and with hearty cheers the ships
are warped into Erebus and Terror Bay, and
arrangements rapidly made to meet the coming
winter of 1845-46.

FRANKLIN'S FIRST WINTER QUARTERS, BEECHEY ISLAND.

CHAPTER IV.

"Oh, though oft depress'd and lonely,
  All *our* fears are laid aside,
If *we* but remember, only
    Such as these have lived and died."
                    LONGFELLOW.

UNDER the friendly shelter of Beechey Island, Franklin and his followers reposed from their arduous labours of 1845, and looked forward confidently to the success which must now attend their efforts in the following year. And they had reason to be confident! Did they not know that, in their remarkable voyage up Wellington Channel and down the new Strait, west of Cornwallis Island, they had explored *three hundred miles* of previously unknown channels leading to the northwest? Could they not point to Cape Walker, and say, " Assuredly it will be an easy task next season to push our ships over the *two hundred and fifty*

E

miles of water which only intervene between Cape
Walker and King William's Land "? Of course
they thought thus. And that their hopes were
fulfilled, though they lived not to wear their
honours, we know, alas! too well. The Polar
winter came in upon them like a giant—it ever
does so. No alternate frost and thaw, sunshine
and gloom, there delays the advent of the winter.
Within the frigid zone each season steps upon sea
and earth to the appointed day, with all its
distinctive characteristics strongly marked. In
one night, winter strikes nature with its mailed
hand, and silence, coldness, death, reign supreme.
The soil and springs are frozen adamant: the
streamlet no longer trickles from aneath the snow-
choked ravines: the plains, slopes, and terraces of
this land of barrenness are clad in winter livery of
dazzling white; the adjacent seas and fiords can
hardly be distinguished from the land, owing to
the uniformity of colour. A shroud of snow
envelopes the stricken region, except where, sharp
and clear against the hard blue sky, stand out the

gaunt mountain precipices of North Devon and the dark and frowning cliffs of Beechey Island—cliffs too steep for even snow-flake to hang upon. There they stand, huge ebon giants, brooding over the land of famine and suffering spread beneath their feet !

Day after day, in rapidly diminishing arcs, the sun at noon approaches the southern edge of the horizon. It is the first week of November, and I see before me a goodly array of officers and men issue from the ship, and proceed to scale the heights of the neighbouring island : they go to bid the bright sun good bye until February 1846. At noon the upper edge of the orb gleams like a beacon-fire for a few minutes over the snow-enveloped shores of North Somerset—and it is gone—leaving them to three months of twilight and darkness. Offering up a silent, fervent prayer for themselves, who were standing there to see that sunset, and for their dear friends in the ice-beset barks at their feet, that they might all be spared to welcome back the life-imparting planet,

we see these pilgrims from the Erebus and Terror,
turn back and descend into the darkness and
gloom, now hanging over their winter quarters.

The tale of energetic battle, with cold privation
and festering monotony has been often told : why
repeat that the officers and men under Franklin in
their first winter within the frozen zone, as nobly
bore the one and cheerfully combated the other ?
The ruins and traces left behind them all attest it.
The observatory, with its double embankment of
earth and stones, its neat finish, and the lavish
expenditure of labour in pavement and pathway :
the shooting gallery under the cliff, the seats
formed of stones, the remains of pleasant picnics in
empty bottles and meat-tins strewed about : the
elaborate cairn upon the north point of Beechey—
a pyramid eight feet high, and at least six feet
long on each side of the base—constructed of old
meat-tins filled with gravel; all tell the same tale
of manful anxiety for physical employment to
distract the mind from suffering and solitude. On
board the ships we picture to ourselves the Arctic

school and theatre: the scholar and dramatist exerting themselves to kill monotony and amuse or instruct their comrades. There are not wanting traces at Cape Riley to show how earnestly the naturalists Goodsir and Stanley laboured to collect specimens: now was their time to arrange and note upon their labours. There is more than one site still visible of tents in which the magnetical observations were obtained: now was the time to record and compare such observations. And, in addition to the charming novelty of a first winter in the frozen sea, the officers in so scientific an expedition had abundance of employment in noting the various phenomena which were daily and hourly occurring around them.

But at length darkness and winter pass away, sunlight and spring return; pale faces again recover their natural rosy tint. Only three of the original party of one hundred and thirty-eight souls have succumbed;* the rest, though thinner,

* All the traces alluded to, as well as those delineated in the accompanying plate, were discovered at and about Beechey

are now inured and hardened to all the changes of the Arctic climate, and exhibit no lack of energy or strength. As soon as the temperature will admit of it, parties are despatched from the ships in various directions with sledges and tents : some have scientific objects in view ; others are directed to try and procure game for their sickly comrades, or to eke out the store of provisions, now reduced to a two years' stock : and, sad it is to record it, nearly all their preserved meats were those of the miscreant Goldner.

Exploratory parties were likewise not wanting ; and those who came on their footsteps in after years saw the signs of their lost comrades' zeal and industry on every side. From Caswell's Tower, which looks towards Lancaster Sound, to Point Innis up Wellington Channel, the marks of camping places and the trails of their sledges were

Island, in 1850-51, by the expeditions under Captain H. Austin, C.B., Captain Penny, and Captain De Haven. The tomb-stones recorded the deaths of two seamen on January 1st and January 4th, 1846, and that of a marine, who died on April 3rd of the same year.

frequent. It was sad to remark, from the form of
their cooking places, and the deep ruts left by their
sledges over the edge of the terraces which abound
in Beechey Island, how little Franklin's people

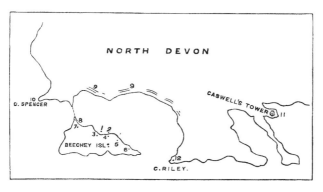

1, 2. Ships.	8. Cairn.
3. Store.	9. Sledge Marks.
4. Graves and Forge.	10. Shooting Gallery.
5. Washing Place.	11. Cairns.
6. Shooting Gallery.	12. Shooting Gallery.
7. Garden.	

TRACES LEFT AT FRANKLIN'S FIRST WINTER QUARTERS IN 1845-6.

were impressed with the importance of rendering
their travelling equipment light and portable, both
as a means of exploration whilst their ships were

imprisoned, and to enable them to escape if their ships were destroyed. The anxiety for their fate expressed by many in Captain Austin's expedition, when remarking upon the fearful expenditure of labour which must have been entailed on Franklin's men in dragging about such sledges as they had evidently had with them, has only been too truly verified. The longest journey made by sledge parties from the Erebus and Terror at Beechey Island, so far as we know, did not exceed *twenty* miles. Franklin's experience of travelling in the Hudson's Bay Territory was evidently at fault in the rugged and desert region in which he was now sojourning; and he had no M'Clintock at his side to show him how, by mechanical skill and careful attention to weights and equipment, sledges might be constructed on which men might carry boats, tents, clothing, food, and fuel, and travel with impunity from February to August, and explore, as he himself has done in that time, nearly fourteen hundred miles of ground or frozen sea. However, no anxieties then pressed on the minds of

those gallant men; "large water" was all they
thought of; give them that, and Behring's Strait
in their ships was still their destination.

The sun has ceased to set, night is as the day,
the snow has long melted off land and floe, the
detached parties have all returned to their ships;
yards are crossed, rigging set up, sails bent, the
graves of their shipmates are neatly paved round,
shells from the bay are prettily arranged over the
sailor's last home by some old messmate. Franklin,
with that Christian earnestness which ever formed
so charming a trait in his character, selects, at the
request of his men, epitaphs which appeal to the
hearts of all, and perhaps no finer picture could be
conceived than that firm and veteran leader leading
his beloved crews on to the perilous execution of
their worldly duty, yet calmly pointing to that text
of Holy Writ in which the prophet warrior of old
reminded his people of their God, " Choose ye this
day whom ye will serve."

The garden on Beechey Island refuses to yield
any vegetables from the seeds so carefully sown in

it; but the officers have brought and transplanted within its border every tuft of saxifrage and pretty anemone and poppy which can be found. The pale pink of the one and delicate straw colour of the other form the only pleasing relief from the monotonous colouring of the barren land. Sportsmen return and declare the game to be too wild for farther sport; but cheer all by saying that the deer and hare have changed their coats from white to russet colour; the ptarmigan's brood have taken wing, the wild duck has long since led her callow young to the open lakes, or off to "holes of water," which are rapidly increasing under cliffs and projecting headlands—all the signs denote that the disruption of the frozen surface of the sea is at hand.

The day of release arrives: in the morning a *black* sky has been seen over the eastern portion of Barrow's Straits, that together with a low barometer indicates a S.E. breeze. The cracks which radiate over the floes in every direction gradually widen, then close again, and form "heavy nips," in

which the fearful pressure occasions a dull grinding
noise. Presently the look-out man on Beechey
Island throws out the signal. The floes are in
motion! A loud hurrah welcomes the joyful signal.
—a race for the point to see the destruction of the
ice. It moves indeed. A mighty agency is at
work; the floe heaves and cracks, now presses fear-
fully in one direction, and then in another; occa-
sionally the awful pressure acting horizontally upon
a huge floe-piece makes it, though ten feet thick,
curve up in a dome-like shape. A dull moaning
is heard as if the very ice cried mercy, and then,
with a sharp report, the mass is shivered into
fragments, hurled up one on top of the other.
Water rapidly shows in all directions, and within
twenty-four hours there is quite as much sea seen
as there was of ice yesterday. Yet the ice-fields
in bays and inlets are still fast; this is the land-
floe, and in that of Beechey Island the ships are
still fast locked; but anticipating such would be
the case, all the spring long men have been carefully sprinkling ashes, sand, and gravel over the

ice in a straight line from the Erebus and Terror to the entrance of the bay. The increased action of the sun upon these foreign substances has occasioned a rapid decay of the floe beneath them, and it only needs a little labour to extricate the expedition.

"Hands, cut out ships!" pipes the hearty boatswain. A hundred strong hands and a dozen ice-saws are soon at work, whilst loud song and merriment awaken the long silent echoes of Beechey Island. The water is reached, the sail is made, the ships cast to the westward, and again they speed towards Cape Walker.

If we open a chart of the Arctic Regions,* it will be observed that *westward* of the Parry Islands, and Baring Island, there is a wide sea whose limits are as yet unknown, and the ice which encumbers it has never yet been traversed by ship, or sledge. All those navigators, Collinson and M'Clure in

---

* Mr. Arrowsmith, of Soho Square, has published an excellent and cheap general map, on a small scale, which will be found very correct.

their ships, and M'Clintock and Mecham with
their sledges, who have with much difficulty and
danger skirted along the southern, and eastern
edge, of this truly frozen sea, mention, in terms of
wonderment, the stupendous thickness and massive
proportions of the vast floes with which it is closely
packed. It was between this truly polar ice and
the steep cliffs of Banks's Land that Sir Robert
M'Clure fairly fought his way in the memorable
voyage of the Investigator. It was in the narrow
and tortuous lane of water left between the low
beach line of North America and the wall of ice
formed by the grounded masses of this fearful pack
that the gallant Collinson carried, in 1852 and
1853, the Enterprise by way of Behring's Strait
to and from the farther shores of Victoria Land;
and it was in the far north-west of the Parry
group that M'Clintock and Mecham, with their
sledges in 1853 gazed, as Parry had done five-and-
thirty years before, with astonishment on that
pack-ice to which all they had seen in the seas
between Prince Patrick's Land and the Atlantic

was a mere bagatelle. It is not that the cold is here more intense, or that the climate is more rigorous, but this accumulation of ponderous ice arises simply from the want of any large direct communication between that portion of the Polar sea and the warm waters of the Pacific and Atlantic Oceans. Behring's Strait is the only vent in a south-westerly direction, and that strait is so shallow that this polar ice (which has been found to draw as much as sixty and eighty feet of water, and to have hummocks upon it of a hundred feet in height), generally grounds in it, until thawed away by the action of the Pacific gulf stream ; and, on the other hand, towards the Atlantic Ocean, the channels, as it will be observed, are most tortuous and much barred with islands. The grand law of nature by which the ice of our Northern Pole is ever flowing towards the torrid zone, holds good, however, within the area to which we are alluding ; and in spite of all obstacles, and although the accumulation of ice every winter exceeds the discharge and destruction, still the action is ever southerly, as in

the seas of Spitzbergen and Nova Zembla. The
slow march of this ice-stream is, however, far
more like that of the ice from some huge parent
glacier than of anything else, for lanes of water, or

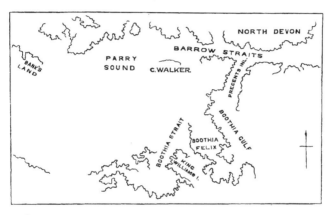

clear spaces of sea, are seldom if ever seen amongst
it; indeed, so compact, so impenetrable is its character, that as yet no navigator has ever succeeded
in crossing any of the ice-streams from this sea of
desolation.

One of these impenetrable ice-streams flows down
between Melville and Banks's Land, and impinging
with fearful force upon the exposed western shores

of Prince of Wales's Land and the islands across Barrow's Straits, curves down what is now called M'Clintock Channel, until it is fairly blocked up in the strait between King William's and Victoria Land. Here the southern edge of the ice-stream comes in contact with the warm waters flowing northward from the rivers of the continent of America, and undergoes a constant and rapid disintegration, the rear of the ice-stream ever pressing forward, yet constantly melted away,* as it reaches the limit which Providence has set upon it.

As Franklin sailed to the west from Beechey Island, he fell upon the edge of this ice-stream in about the longitude of Cape Walker; then to the west of it, and of Lowther, Young, and Hamilton Islands, he observed the floes being broken up, and rapidly disintegrated by meeting the warm waters of Barrow's Straits; but within and amongst that pack there could have been no hope of a

---

* Taking the drift of the lost Erebus and Terror from September, 1846, to April, 1848, as our guide, this ice-stream moves at about the rate of a mile-and-a-half in a month.

passage, whilst on the other hand the ridges of pressed-up shingle and off-lying shoals round the land west of Cape Walker threatened destruction to the Erebus and Terror if they attempted that route; whereas, as far as they could look southward between Capes Walker and Bunny, there stretched away a fair and promising channel leading direct to the American continent, and with ice in it of no very aged appearance. Who that has stood as they did on Cape Walker, can doubt which route Franklin preferred under such circumstances?

The middle of August and a fortnight of navigation are before them. "A lead! a lead! and large water! away to the south," calls the ice-master from the crow's nest; and from under the friendly shelter of Cape Walker the expedition bears away, and they progress a-pace down what we know as Peel's Channel. On the eastern hand rise the steep black cliffs of North Somerset, cut here and there with deep cleft and snow-filled ravine; along the base a ridge of ice is piled up full forty feet high; it gleams in white and blue against the granite

F

cliff, and is reflected in the calm waters of an
Arctic summer's day—how still, how calm, how
sublimely grand—but the experienced seaman is not
beguiled by the deceptive beauty of such a scene,
but thinks of the dark and stormy nights when,
and that before many short days are past, the
north-west hurricane will again launch against
those cliffs, the ice-fields of Melville Strait.   On the
western hand, the sandstone cliffs, and the sheltered
coves of Prince of Wales's Land, have donned
their brightest looks, and siren-like, lure the discoverer, by many an unexplored bay and fiord, to
delay awhile and visit them.   It may not be; the
Erebus and Terror press on, for Cape Herschel of
King William's Land and the American continent
are ahead—they are fast nearing it ?   Once there,
they will have discovered the long-sought North-
West Passage !   They will have done that " one
thing whereby great minds may become notable."
Two degrees of latitude are passed over : the passage
contracts ; for awhile it looks as if they were in a
cul-de-sac ; islands locked in with one another

excite some anxiety for a channel. The two ships are close to each other, the eager officers and men crowd gunwale and tops. Hepburn Island bars the way : they round it. Hurrah, hurrah ! the path opens before them, the lands on either recede, as sea, an open sea, is before them. They dip their ensigns, and cheer each other in friendly congratulation : joy, joy ! another one hundred miles, and King William's Land will rise in view. The prize is now within their grasp, whatever be the cost.

The sailors' prayer for open water is, however, only granted in a limited sense, for directly the coast of Prince of Wales's Island is lost to view, and that they are no longer shielded by land to the west, the great ice-stream from Melville Island again falls upon it. The Erebus and Terror pass a channel leading into Regent's Inlet, our Bellot Channel; they advance down the edge of that ice-stream as far as latitude 71°. The only passage to the coast of America that Franklin knows of, is now nearly south-west of his position, it leads between King William's and Victoria Land. For, alas! in his chart King William's Land [see p. 31] was represented to be connected with Boothia by a deep bay, called Poet's Bay. It is true that to the south-west the hopeless looking ice-stream bars his way, and that to the south-east the road looks clear and promising; but then, did not his chart say that there was no channel east of King William's Land, by which to reach the American shore? There was no alternative, they must enter the pack or ice-stream, and go with it to the south-west.

Had they not already passed over two-hundred out of the three hundred miles between Cape Walker and Cape Herschel? Were they the men to flinch from a struggle for the remaining hundred miles? That struggle commenced as the winter closed in, and just as King William's Land was in sight the Erebus and Terror became beset, and eventually fixed for the winter of 1846-7, in latitude 70° 5' north, and longitude 98° 23' west, about twelve miles due north of Cape Felix. More

IN THE ICE-STREAM OFF CAPE FELIX.

dangerous and unpromising winter-quarters could hardly have fallen to their lot, but they were helpless in that ice-stream.   Sixteen years previously Sir James Ross had stood upon Cape Felix.   He travelled on foot in the early spring of 1830, from Victoria Harbour in the Gulf of Boothia, and explored the northern coast of King William's Land, and standing on the 29th of May on this very Cape Felix, remarked with astonishment, the fearful nature of the oceanic ice, which was pressed upon the shores ; and he mentions that in some places the pressure had driven the floes inland, half a mile beyond the highest tide-mark !   Such the terrible winter-quarters of those lone barks and their gallant crews ; and if that season of monotony and hardship was trying to them in Beechey Island, where they could in some measure change the scene by travelling in one direction or the other, how infinitely more so it must have been with nothing round them but ice-hummock and floe-piece, with the ships constantly subjected to pressure and ice-nip, and the crews often threatened during the depth of winter with the probability of having their ships swallowed up in an Arctic tempest, when the ice-fields would rear and crush themselves one against the other under the influence of the awful pressure from the north-west.

The God of storms, who thus lashed the wintry north with His might, shielded however those brave men; and now, inured to the dangers of icy seas, they slept and laboured not less pleasantly because the floes were rocking their wooden homes; and consoled themselves that they were only then ninety miles from Cape Herschel, and that even a sledge party could reach it next spring (1847) before the navigation would be open.

Thus their second winter passes. King William's Land shows out here and there from its winter livery; for evaporation serves to denude those barren lands of snow long before any thaw takes place. May comes in; the unsetting sun in dazzling splendour pours its flood of perpetual light over the broken, shattered blocks of ice which form this truly polar ice-stream; drops of water

trickle down the sides of the weather-beaten ships,
and icicles hang pendant from the edge of hummocks; yet it is still intensely cold in the shade.
Lieutenant Graham Gore, and Mr. F. Des Vœux,
mate, both of the Erebus, are about to leave the
ships for the land. They have six men with them.
Why do all grasp them so fervently by the hand?
Why do even the sick come up to give them a
parting cheer? Surely they went forth to bring
back the assurance that the expedition was really
in the direct channel leading to those waters traversed in former years by Franklin; and to tell
them all that they really were the discoverers of
the long-sought passage! A record was left
by Gore and Des Vœux, in a cairn beyond Cape
Victory, on the west coast of King William's
Land; it tells us that, "on May 24th, 1847, all
were well on board the ships, and that Sir John
Franklin still commanded." Graham Gore probably traversed the short distance between his
cairn and that on Cape Herschel in a week; and
we can fancy him and the enthusiastic Des Vœux,

casting one glance upon the long-sought shores of America, and hastening back to share their delight with those imprisoned in the ships.

Alas! why do their shipmates meet the flushed travellers with sorrow imprinted on pale countenances! Why, as they cheer at the glad tidings they bring, does the tear suffuse the eye of these rough and hardy men? Their chief lies on his death-bed; a long career of honour and of worth is drawing to its close. The shout of victory, which cheered the last hour of Nelson and of Wolfe, rang not less heartily round the bed of the gallant Franklin, and lit up that kind eye with its last gleam of triumph. Like them, his last thought must have been of his country's glory, and the welfare of those whom he well knew must now hope in vain for his return.

A toll for the brave—the drooping ensigns of England trail only half-mast; officers and men with sad faces walk lightly, as if they feared to disturb the mortal remains of him they love so much. The solemn peal of the ship's bell reverberates amongst

BURIAL OF SIR JOHN FRANKLIN.

the masses of solid ice; a group of affectionate followers stand round a huge chasm amongst the ice-stream, and Fitzjames, who had sworn only to part from him in death, reads the service for the dead over the grave of Franklin.

Oh! mourn him not, seamen and brother Englishmen! unless ye can point to a more honourable end or a nobler grave. Like another Moses, he fell when his work was accomplished, with the long object of his life in view. Franklin, the discoverer of the North-west Passage, had his Pisgah, and so long as his countrymen shall hold dear disinterested devotion and gallant perseverance in a good cause, so long shall they point to the career and fate of this gallant sailor.

* * * * * * *

The autumn comes. It is not without anxiety that Crozier and Fitzjames contemplate the prospect before them; but they keep those feelings to themselves. The Pacific is far off; the safe retreat of their men up the Great Fish River, or Copper-

mine, is fraught with peril, unless their countrymen
at home have established depôts of provisions at
their embouchures; and, worse still, their provisions fail next year, and scurvy is already showing
itself amongst the crews. At last the ice-stream
moves—it swings to and fro—the vessels are
thrown into one position of danger and then
another. Days elapse—ah! they count the hours
before winter will assuredly come back; and how
they pray for water—water to float the ships in;
only one narrow lane through this hard-hearted
pack—one narrow lane for ninety miles, and they
are saved! but if not *   *   *   *   Thy will be
done!

The ice-stream moves south—but slowly; the
men fear to remark to each other how slowly; the
slide of a glacier down the Alpine pass is scarcely
less perceptible. Yet it *does* move south, and they
look to heaven and thank their God. Ten miles,
twenty miles, are passed over, still beset; not a foot
of open water in sight, yet still they drift to the
south. Thirty miles are now accomplished; they

have only sixty miles of ice between them and the
sea, off the American coast—nay, less; for only let
them get round that west extreme of King William's
Land, which is seen projecting into the ice-stream,
and they are saved !

September, 1847, has come in.   The new ice is
forming fast; the drift of the ice-stream diminishes,
—can it have stopped ?   Mercy ! mercy !   It sways
to and fro ;—gaunt, scurvy-stricken men watch the
daily movement with bated breath ; the ships have
ceased to drift; they are now fifteen miles north of
Cape Victory.   God, in his mercy, shield those
gallant crews !   The dread winter of 1847-48
closes around these forlorn and now desperate men ;
—disease and scurvy, want and cold, now indeed
press them heavily.   Brave men are suffering ; we
will not look upon their sore trial.

The sun of 1848 rises again upon the imprisoned
expedition, and never did it look down on a nobler
yet sadder sight.   Nine officers and twelve men
have perished during the past season of trial ; the
survivors, one hundred and four in number, are

assembled round their leaders—Crozier and Fitzjames—a wan, half-starved crew.   Poor souls, they
are going to escape for their lives by ascending the
Great Fish River.   Fitzjames, still vigorous, con-
ceals his fears of ever saving so many in the hunger-
stricken region they have to traverse.   As the
constant friend and companion of Franklin, he
knows but too well from the fearful experiences of
his lamented chief, what toil, hardship, and want,
await them before a country capable of supporting
life can be reached.   All that long last winter, has
he pored over the graphic and touching tale of
Franklin's overland journeys in Arctic America,
and culled but small hope ; yet he knows there is
no time for despondency ; the men look to their
officers for hope and confidence at such a juncture,
and shall he be wanting at such a crisis ?   No,
assuredly not ; and he strives hard, by kind and
cheering words, to impart new courage to many a
drooping heart.   The fresh preserved provisions on
board the ships have failed ; salted meat is simply
poison to the scurvy-stricken men ; they must quit

the ships or die; and, if they must die, is it not better that they should do so making a last gallant struggle for life?—at any rate, they can leave their bleaching skeletons as a monument upon Cape Herschel, of having successfully done their duty.

They pile up then their sledges with all description of gear; for as yet they know not how much their strength has diminished. Each ship's company brings a large whale-boat which has been carefully fitted upon a sledge; in them the sick and disabled are tenderly packed; each man carries a great quantity of clothing. Care is taken to have plenty of guns, powder, and shot; for they can drag at the utmost but forty days' provisions with them, and at the expiration of that time they hope to be in a country where their guns will feed them. Every trinket and piece of silver in the ships is carefully divided amongst the men; they intend to conciliate the natives with these baubles, or to procure food; and so far as foresight could afford the party every hope of safety, all has been done. But one fatal error occurred,—the question of weight to be dragged, with diminished physical power, has never been taken into consideration; or, if considered, no proper remedy applied.

On the 22nd of April, 1848, these gallant men fell into the drag-ropes of their sledges and boats; the colours were hoisted on their dear old ships, three hearty cheers were given for the stout craft that had borne them so nobly through many perils, and without a blush, for there was no cause for it, at deserting her Majesty's ships Erebus and Terror, Captains Crozier and Fitzjames lead the road to the nearest point of land, named Cape Victory.* Poor souls, they were three days traversing the intervening distance of fifteen miles, and the sad conviction was already pressing upon them, that they had over-estimated their physical strength and powers of endurance. Around the large cairn erected upon Point Victory the shivering diseased men cast away everything that

* So called by Captain Sir James Ross in his exploration of 1830. It was the farthest point reached on King William's Land by that distinguished Arctic traveller.

could be spared; indeed perhaps much that, at that inclement season, they still needed to shield their half-starved frames from the biting blast. Pick-axes, shovels, rope, blocks, clothing, stores of all sorts, except provisions, sextants, quadrants, oars, and even a medicine-case, expressly fitted up for the journey, were here thrown away. Unrolling the record left here in the previous year by the good and gallant Gore, Captain Fitzjames proceeded to write round its margin those few—alas ! too few —but graphic words, which tell us all we shall ever know of this last sad page in their touching history. The ink had to be thawed by fire, and benumbed must the hand have been that wrote those words; yet the writing is that of the same firm, self-reliant, light-hearted man, who, three short years previously, had been noted at Green-hithe as the life of the expedition.

In spite of frostbites and fatigue, the party presses on. They *must* keep marching southward towards the mainland where they hope to find deer and salmon, for upon their sledges they have only got forty days' provision, and that store will be expended by the 7th of June, at latest.* How are they to live after that? is a sad thought which flashes across the mind of many. They sigh, but will not impart their anxieties to each other. Seamen-like, the light joke and merry laugh still flash from mouth to mouth, and seem for the while to lighten the poor heart of its load of misery.

Poor lost ones! we mark them day by day growing weaker under the fearful toil of dragging such ponderous sledges and boats, as well as their disabled comrades, through the deep snow, and over rugged ice; we hear the cheering appeal of the gallant officers to the despairing ones, the kind

---

* It is well known by the experience of Arctic travellers that forty days is the maximum quantity of food, in addition to other weights, that the best-equipped party could have dragged on their sledges; and as the Great Fish River was known not to open before August, it must have been dire necessity alone that induced Crozier and Fitzjames to quit their ships at so early a period of the year, that nearly six weeks must have intervened between the expenditure of the provisions upon their sledges and the disruption of the ice upon the Great Fish River.

applause heartily bestowed to the self-sacrificing
and the brave.   Bodily endurance has its limits,
devotion to one's brother man its bounds, and half-
way between Cape Victory where they landed and
Cape Herschel, it becomes apparent that if any are
to be saved there must be a division of the party,
and that the weak and disabled must stay behind,
or return to the ships.   One of the large boats is
here turned with her bow northward ; some stay
here, the rest push on.   Of those who thus remained, or tried to return, all we know is, that in
long years afterwards, two skeletons were found in
that boat, and that the wandering Esquimaux found
on board one ship, the bones of another " large man
with big bones," as they described him.   On the
fate of the rest of the sick and weak—and they
must have formed a large proportion of the original
party of 106 souls that landed on Cape Victory—
we need not dwell.

The rest push on : they have tried to cheer their
shipmates with the vain hope that they will yet
return to save them—vain hope !   Yet we see

them with bending bodies, and with the sweat-drops freezing upon their pallid faces, straining every nerve to save sweet life—they pass from sight into the snow-storm, which the warm south wind kindly sends to shroud the worn-out ones, who gently lie down to die; and they died so peacefully, so calmly, with the mind sweetly wandering back to the homes and friends of their childhood; the long-remembered prayer upon their lips, and their last fleeting thoughts of some long-treasured love for one they would one day meet in Heaven. The cairn on Cape Herschel was reached—no one had been there since "Dease and Simpson" in 1839, except themselves. Here the last record was placed of their success and sad position, and then this forlorn hope of desperate men pushed on towards the Great Fish River; and, if we needed any proof of Franklin's Expedition having been the "first to discover the North-West Passage," or of the utter extremity to which this retreating party was reduced, we need but point to the bleaching skeleton which lies a few miles southward of Cape Herschel;

that silent witness has been accorded us, and he
still lies as he fell, on his face, with his head
towards his home.   His comrades had neither
turned, nor buried him.   But why pursue the
subject further ; why attempt to lift the veil with
which the All Merciful has been pleased to shut
out from mortal ken the last sad hour of brave men
battling with famine and disease.

All we know farther of this " forlorn hope " is
that Dr. Rae, from Esquimaux report, states that
about *forty* white men were seen early one spring,
dragging a boat and sledges south upon, or near,
King William's Land.   The men were thin, and
supposed to be getting short of provisions; the
party was led by a stout middle-aged man.   Later
in the season, after the arrival of the wild fowl
(May), but before the ice broke up, the bodies of
thirty persons, and some graves, were discovered on
the continent, and five other corpses on an island ;
some of these bodies were in a tent, others under
the boat, which had been turned over to afford
shelter.   Of those corpses seen on the island, one

was supposed to be a chief; he had a telescope over his shoulders, and a double-barrelled gun beneath him. The native description of the locality where this sad scene was discovered agreed exactly with Montreal Island and Point Ogle, at the entrance of the Great Fish River; and knowing what we now do of the position of the ships, and date of abandonment, and taking all circumstances into consideration, it is now vain to suppose that any survivors exist of the crews of the Erebus and Terror; nor is it likely that records of their voyage will now be found, as we may be assured that no Christian officers or men would for one moment think of dragging logs, books, or journals with them when they were obliged to abandon their dying comrades on King William's Land: and, indeed, when it is remembered that they neither *cached* journals or books of any description at Cape Victory, or the deserted boat, it is not probable that any were ever taken out of the vessels at a juncture when the sole object must have been to save life—and life only.

We will now briefly relate how a woman's devoted love, and a generous nation's sympathy, at last cleared up the mystery which once hung over the voyage of Her Majesty's ships Erebus and Terror, and secured to Franklin and his followers the honour for which they died—that of being the *First Discoverers of the North-West Passage.*

CHAPTER V.

THE SEARCH FOR FRANKLIN.

———◆———

" A lady with a lamp shall stand
In the great history of the land,
A noble type of good
Heroic womanhood."

LONGFELLOW.

In 1848 the public alarm at the long-continued absence of Franklin's Expedition occasioned the search to be commenced. The sympathy for the missing ones not only extended to every class of Great Britain, but spread to Europe as well as America. The action of the British Admiralty not being considered sufficiently energetic, private expeditions were set on foot. Lady Franklin, in England, and the munificent American, Mr. Grinnell, were the prime movers in either country. Those men of science, and those who, anxious to secure their country the palm of maritime discovery, had encouraged the sending forth of the Franklin Expedition, were in no wise remiss in pressing the Admiralty to persist in every effort to save the ill-starred crews. Sir John Barrow and his son did all that men could do. The Royal Society, and especially their talented secretary, Colonel Sabine; Thomas Brown, the Linnæus of England, who had sailed with Franklin when a boy, in Flinders' expedition to Australia; the great Humboldt, whose anxiety for further magnetical observations had much contributed to the despatch of Franklin's Expedition; ay, even crowned heads, represented by our own much loved Sovereign and the beautiful Empress of the French, expressed a warm interest, and stimulated the great cry of rescue which went through this earnest land.

The royal and mercantile navies of Britain offered hundreds of volunteers, ready to devote themselves to the chivalrous task of seeking and striving to save their missing countrymen. Expedition after expedition was sent for eleven long years, and although it was not ordained that any

of Franklin's Expedition should be rescued, yet we
have now the satisfaction of knowing the history of
their wonderful voyage, and feel that we have done
our duty as a nation in having lifted the veil of
mystery which once hung over their sad but
glorious fate. Those who were first sent into those
frozen seas knew no more than Franklin did on
leaving England, of the geography of the vast
region between Lancaster Sound and Behring's
Strait; and in all that area, many tens of thousands of square miles, they had to seek two atoms
—two ships. The labour was long and disheart-
ening; and, with the exception of the discovery in
1850 of Franklin's winter quarters of 1845-46,
under Beechey Island, no clue to their whereabouts
was found until near the fall of 1854. That discovery at Beechey Island merely assured us that he
was within the area above alluded to, and that his
expedition had not perished, as some supposed, in
Baffin's Bay. During those six years, however,
the entire geography of the regions of Arctic
America was made known; and, with the exception

of a small portion around King William's Land, every coast, creek, and harbour thoroughly searched. A comparison of the two charts we have given, will best prove how much of this area was thus laid open. It was the accomplishment of these explorations by the successive expeditions of Sir James Ross, Richardson, Rae, Austin, Penny, De Haven, Belcher, Collinson, M'Clure, and their gallant associates, that enabled Captain M'Clintock, as he very justly remarks, to confine his operations to a spot which, though last searched, has happily proved to be the right one. It should be remembered, that these explorations were nearly all made by our seamen and officers on foot, dragging sledges, on which were piled tents, provision, fuel for cooking, and raiment. This sledging was brought to perfection by Captain M'Clintock. He made one foot journey in those regions with Sir James Ross in 1848 with the equipment then known to Arctic navigators, and such as Franklin probably had, and was struck with its imperfections, and the total impossibility of making long journeys with *matériel* so clumsy, and entailing so much unnecessary labour upon the seamen. His suggestions were subsequently eagerly adopted, and in some cases improved upon by others; the consequence was, that whereas in 1848 we found our sledge-parties able to remain away from the frozen-in ships only forty days to explore two hundred miles of coast, those of Captain Horatio Austin's expedition were away for eighty days, and went over eight hundred miles of ground. And in Sir Edward Belcher's expedition the journeys extended over a hundred and odd days, and distances were accomplished of nearly 1400 miles!

In spite of these improvements, the labour and hardship entailed upon our seamen by these sledge-journeys remained extremely severe; and none but those who have witnessed it can conceive the constant suffering it entailed upon our men, or the unflagging zeal and earnestness with which they underwent it year after year, in the hope of discovering their lost countrymen. There were two

points to be ascertained by the officers conducting
the search, in order to insure the utmost possible
amount of work being done each season : the one
was the maximum weight a strong man could drag
through deep snow and over heavy ice for a con-
secutive number of days ; the other was, to what
temperature we could safely expose them, and
upon how small a quantity of food.

The results obtained were curious. The maximum weight was ascertained to be 220 lb. per
man ; and of that weight 3 lb. per diem was consumed by each man for food and fuel—viz., 1 lb. of
bread, 1 lb. of meat, while the other pound com-
prised his spirits, tea, cocoa, sugar, tobacco, and
fuel for cooking. Upon this estimate it was found
that, for a hundred days' journey, they could
march ten miles per diem, and endure a temperature with impunity of fifty or sixty degrees below
the freezing-point of water. These facts we offer
for the information of military authorities ; and
they should remember, that our men dragged their
tents with them, and that the country traversed

was one vast desert, affording only water, though that had to be thawed from snow, out of the daily modicum of fuel.

All this labour, however—all this generous expenditure of the legislature of England on behalf of her people, who entered deeply and earnestly into the sad question, What has become of Franklin?—brought back no information of his fate : and still further to test the perseverance which forms the best trait of our national character, the fall of 1854 witnessed the abandonment in icy seas of a noble expedition of four ships. It was indeed a catastrophe, though neither an officer nor a man was lost. The "I told you so" rang through the land of those who had long since got rid of the question by tumbling icebergs over on top of the Erebus and Terror ; and those who felt convinced that the mystery would yet be unravelled, sighed, and knew not where to look for support. The skill and hardihood of the officers—the devotion and zeal of our sailors, and the accomplishment of the North-West Passage by Captain Sir Robert

M'Clure—were accepted by the public as some consolation for the wounded maritime pride of Britain in the inconclusive allied war with Russia, though it was decided that no further search should be made on the part of the Government.

Hardly had men declared the solution of the fate of the lost expedition a hopeless task, when in October, 1854, from the shores of Prince Regent's Inlet appeared a traveller, Dr. Rae, bringing the information which we mentioned in the end of the last chapter, of the starvation of a forlorn hope of forty men and officers from the Erebus and Terror, at the mouth of the Great Fish River. The Esquimaux from whom he obtained his intelligence, told him that the two ships had been beset or wrecked, off the coast of King William's Land.

The lost expedition was thus reported to be in the centre of the square of unsearched ground, before alluded to. It would have been far more easily accessible to our various expeditions, whether by way of Barrow or Behring's Strait, than many of the more remote regions explored by them ; but,

by a strange fatality, all our travellers turned back
short of the goal, because they found no cairn, no
trace, no record to induce them to push on towards
it. However, that there the lost ships were, no one
who knew anything of the matter could then doubt;
and of course the natural conclusion under such
circumstances was, that some one of the Arctic
ships in our dockyards would have been immediately sent to close the search in a satisfactory
manner, even though all hope of saving life might
be at an end. The Admiralty and Government
thought otherwise; all public endeavours ceased;
and, as is too often the case in Britain, private enterprise was left to crown the column which the
devotion of a public profession had served to erect.
At this juncture, the widow of Franklin stepped
forth to carry out what the admirals in Whitehall
and statesmen in Downing Street declared to be an
impossibility. This energetic, self-reliant woman,
seconded by a few staunch friends, pre-eminent
amongst whom stood Sir Roderick Murchison, proceeded for the third time to try to carry out by

private means what ignorance, rather than ill-will, prevented the Admiralty from executing, for, after the death of Barrow and Beaufort, and the retirement of Admiral Hamilton, as well as Barrow's son, the only person left at the Board who understood the question was Admiral Sir Alexander Milne, and he stood alone in voting for a final Government expedition. Lady Franklin's plan was to send a single vessel down from Prince Regent's Inlet, or Cape Walker, towards King William's Land. Twice already had she been foiled in this identical scheme; though on the last occasion the discovery of Bellot's Strait by Captain Kennedy, leading direct to King William's Land, paved the way for her final effort.

An appeal to the public for pecuniary aid met with but partial success, and Lady Frankin had to sacrifice all her available property and live humbly in lodgings, to enable her to meet the necessary expenses attendant on the purchase of a fine screw schooner yacht, the Fox, and her equipment for Arctic service. Many able officers of the naval and mercantile marine came generously forward and volunteered their gratuitous services. Amongst the first was Captain George H. Richards; but hardly had his offer been accepted, when the Admiralty appointed him to the Plumper for a survey of Vancouver's Land. His place was almost immediately filled by Captain Leopold M'Clintock, whose high reputation during years of continuous service in those frozen seas rendered his acquisition an omen of perfect success.

Various circumstances combined to retard the departure of the gallant little Fox, and it was not until July, 1857, that she and her noble company put forth from Aberdeen. Round Captain M'Clintock stood twenty-five gallant men, including three officers and an interpreter. Allen Young, a generous captain, of whom the merchant service have good reason to be proud, went as sailing master, and not only gave his services gratuitously, but threw £500 into the general fund for expenses. Lieutenant Hobson of the Navy, served as chief officer, and Dr. Walker of Belfast, a young and

rising medical man, went also to seek honour where
so many of his gallant countrymen had already
won it. Petersen, the Dane, who had spent half
his life within the Arctic zone, quitted Copenhagen
at an hour's notice to aid Captain M'Clintock as
Esquimaux interpreter; and amongst the men
were many gallant fellows who had for years
laboured under Her Majesty's pendant in the frozen
north.

The Fox before long reached the edge of that
vast belt of broken-up ice which all the summer
stretches across the upper portion of Baffin's Bay,
and is known under the general term of middle-ice.
M'Clintock was late, the season unfavourable, his
vessel a small one, yet he fought a gallant fight to
make his way to Lancaster Sound. Repulsed in
one quarter, we see him doubling back to another,
the tiny Fox struggling with a sea of ice-fields and
icebergs—stout hearts and strong hands carrying
her and her company through many a hair-breadth
escape. The middle-ice, however, is too strong for
them. In an unlucky hour they are imprisoned,

H

ice surrounds them, water even in holes becomes daily less, winter sweeps down from her dreary home, and all that vast sea of broken ice becomes frozen together. They are beset for the winter, and must go with the ice wherever it pleases. Twenty-five men in a tiny craft drifting throughout that long dark winter, in the midst of icebergs and pack-ice, which ever roll from the Pole to the Equator, was a strange and solemn spectacle. The calm and modest endurance of their six months' trial, as told by the gallant leader, is a thing to make one proud that such as they are our countrymen.

Late in April, 1858, the Fox may again be seen; she has approached the open sea; a furious storm arises, sending huge rollers under the ice, which heaves and rears on all sides. A battle for life commences between the stout yacht and the charging floes. Under sail and steam, she works out against all obstacles, and, thanks to a taper bow, escapes the destruction which would infallibly have overtaken a vessel of bluffer build. The sea is sighted, and eventually entered; all on board the Fox are well,—all in good spirits,—one of the company has alone perished by an accident. Fortune ever smiles upon the resolute, and the middle-ice no longer barred the road to Lancaster Sound; by the end of July the Fox had reached its entrance. The hardy whaling-men of Aberdeen and Hull, who had just returned to their fishing-ground from home, cheered the little craft on with many a hearty "God speed ye!" and shared with those on board the Fox their luxuries of frozen fresh beef and vegetables. Beyond the haunts of whale-fishermen, and beyond those even of the still hardier Esquimaux, the Fox must press on. Beechey Island is reached, and from the depôt of provisions left there by government expeditions, the now diminished stock of the schooner is replenished; and, favoured by an extraordinarily open season, Captain M'Clintock was able to reach Cape Walker, and pass down Peel Strait towards King William's Land, until brought up, on August 17th, by fixed ice, at a point twenty-five miles within its entrance. Baffled, but not disheartened, Captain M'Clintock bethought himself of the route suggested by Lady Franklin, by way of Prince Regent's Inlet and Bellot Strait; and with that decision which, combined with sound judgment, forms the most valuable qualification of an Arctic navigator, he immediately retraced his steps, and by the 20th, or three days later, was at the eastern entrance of Bellot Strait, watching for a chance to push through it into the western sea around King William's Land.

The scene in that strait was enough to daunt men less accustomed to such dangers. On either hand precipitous walls of granite, topped by mountains ever covered with snow, whilst to and fro, in the space between them, the ice was grinding and churning with great violence under the influence of a fierce tide. Like a terrier at a rat-hole, the staunch Fox waited for an opportunity to run the gauntlet through this strait. This perseverance was partially rewarded, for on the 6th September they were able to reach its western entrance, though

THE "FOX" IN HARBOUR.

again to be brought up by a belt of fixed ice which stretched across the path, and was held together by some islands named the Tasmania Group. The winter of 1858-59 now set in, and, much to the chagrin of those on board the Fox, all hope of reaching the western sea had to be abandoned, although separated from them only by an ice-field six miles wide. An unusually cold and stormy winter had now to be endured by men debilitated by a previous winter in the packed ice of Baffin's Bay; and the resources of Boothia Felix yielded them in fresh food only eight reindeer, two bears, and eighteen seals. Against these privations, however, there was a feeling of perfect confidence that the returning spring would enable them to march to King William's Land, and solve the mystery.

On February 17th, Captain M'Clintock and Captain Young left the Fox to establish advanced depôts of provision for the summer sledge parties, a necessary measure, which Lieutenant Hobson had been nearly lost in attempting to accomplish in

the previous autumn. M'Clintock went south
towards the Magnetic Pole, and Young westerly
for Prince of Wales's Land. On the 15th March
they both returned to the Fox, somewhat cut up
by the intense cold and privation; but the cheers
which rang through the little craft told that a clue
had indeed been obtained to the fate of the Erebus
and Terror. M'Clintock had met forty-five Esquimaux, and, during a sojourn of four days amongst
them, had learnt that " several years ago a ship
was crushed by the ice off the north shore of King
William's Land, and her people landed and went
away to the Great Fish River, where they died."
These natives had a quantity of wood from a boat
left by the " starving white men " on the Great
River. The impatience of all on board the Fox to
start with their sledges to the westward may be
easily understood. The Esquimaux mentioning
only one ship as having been sunk, gave rise to the
hope that the other vessel would be found, and
obliged Captain M'Clintock to detach a party under
Captain Young towards Prince of Wales's Land,

whilst he and Lieutenant Hobson went south for King William's Land and the Fish River.

On the 2nd of April the three officers left the ship with a man-sledge and a dog-sledge to each. Of Captain Young we may say that he made a most successful and lengthy journey, connecting the unexplored coast-lines of all the land to the northward and westward, and correcting its position, but without finding a single cairn or record left by Franklin. Captain M'Clintock and Hobson went together as far as the Magnetic Pole, and, before parting company, gathered from some natives that the second vessel, hitherto unaccounted for, had been drifted on shore by the ice in the fall of the same year that the other ship was crushed. Captain M'Clintock undertook to go down the east side of King William's Land direct to the Fish River, and taking up the clue which Dr. Rae's report and Mr. Anderson's journey to Montreal Island in 1855 afforded him, follow it whither it led. Hobson had to cross to the North Cape of King William's Land, and push down the west coast as far as possible.

Captain M'Clintock, when half-way down the east coast of King William's Land, met a party of Esquimaux who had been, in 1857, at the wreck spoken of by their countrymen. Their route to her had been across King William's Land, and they readily bartered away all the articles taken out of her. An intelligent old woman said that it was in the fall of the year that the ship was forced on shore; that the starving white men had fallen on their way to the Great River, and that their bodies were found by her countrymen in the following winter. She told that, on board the wrecked ship, there was one dead white man,—"a tall man with long teeth and large bones." There had been "at one time many books on board of her, as well as other things; but all had been taken away or destroyed when she was last at the wreck."

The destruction of one ship and the wreck of the other appeared, so far as M'Clintock could ascertain, to have occurred subsequently to their abandonment. No Esquimaux that were met had ever before seen a living white man; and, although great

thieves, they appeared to be in nowise alarmed at
Captain M'Clintock or his men. From this party
the gallant captain pushed on for Montreal Island;
but he found nothing more than Anderson had
reported; and in a careful sweep of the shores
about Point Ogle and Barrow Island he was equally
unsuccessful.

Returning to King William's Land, he now
struck along the south-western shores, in the hope
of discovering the wreck spoken of by the natives at
Cape Norton. She must, however, have been
swept away by the ice in 1858, or sunk, for no
signs of her could be discovered. The Esquimaux
had evidently carried off every trace left by the
retreating party between Cape Herschel and Montreal Island, except the skeleton of one man ten
miles south of Cape Herschel, and the remains of
a plundered cairn on the Cape itself. The skeleton
lay exactly as the famished seaman had fallen,
with his head toward the Great Fish River, and
his face to the ground; and those who fancy that
Fitzjames or Crozier would still have dragged log-

books and journals to that river, must explain away
the charge of common humanity which such an
hypothesis involves, when they appeared not to
have had time to turn over, much less to bury,
their perishing comrades.

Beyond the western extremity of King William's
Land, the Esquimaux appeared not to have
travelled, and from thence to Cape Felix the beach
was strewn with the wreck of that disastrous
retreat of Franklin's people, of which we endea-
voured in an earlier chapter to convey some idea.

There were one or two observations made by
Captain M'Clintock and his Lieutenant that are
full of deep meaning to those conversant with
Arctic exploration. In the first place, none of
those coloured tins, in which preserved fresh meat
is usually packed, were found anywhere along the
trail of Franklin's crews, even at what appeared to
be a station for magnetical observation in 1847, at
which officers and men must necessarily have been
encamped for a considerable period. All relics of
their food, such as bones, indicated that *salt meat*

must have been their principal sustenance at this period, and such a dietary would have been certain death by scurvy to the unfortunate men, whose stock of preserved provisions had apparently become expended, or been found to be unfit for food, as most of the meats supplied to the navy at that period were found to be in other quarters of the globe. Had Franklin's parties had such meat-tins with them, they would infallibly have been found, for they abounded on the trail of their sledges about Beechey Island; and later Arctic travellers have left similar traces of their journeyings behind them, which will be recognised for many years to come by any visitors to the localities they have wandered over.

Another fact was noticed, and that was the total absence of all reserve stores of *provisions*, whether salted or fresh, although there was abundance of clothing left at Point Victory. This leads to the inference that they really had had none on board their ships, except what they could drag with them on their sledges, which we know could not have been more than was equal to *forty days'* consumption. Had there been food on board, it seems the height of improbability that Crozier and Fitzjames would, in the first place, have abandoned their ships so long before the Great Fish River was likely to break open, and equally strange that they should not have had the foresight to make a cache of provisions in store, where it would be safe from the risk of shipwreck, to which the Erebus and Terror became doubly liable after the officers and men had abandoned them.

All this, we think, points to two grand facts : that, in the first place, their preserved meats had long been consumed, or become unfit for consumption ; and that, in the second place, *they quitted the ships because all their salt meat and provisions were expended.* Lieutenant Hobson had of course forestalled Captain M'Clintock in the discoveries made here ; but what with the search made by that officer both on his outward and homeward march, as well as that subsequently carried out by Captain M'Clintock over the same ground, there cannot be

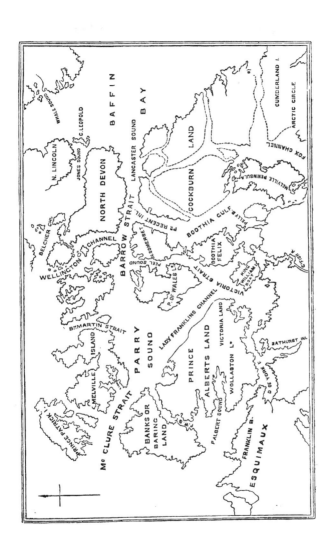

much reason to suppose that any undiscovered
documents exist; and all who know anything of
those regions will agree with Captain M'Clintock in
believing that all hope is now at an end of finding
any one living of the unfortunate crews of the
Erebus and Terror. With respect to the existence
of abundance of animal life on King William's Land,
the fact that only forty natives in all were found
living on that island by Captain M'Clintock ought
to be pretty conclusive: the Esquimaux would take
care to be in any such Arctic paradise; and, further-
more, had game been plentiful anywhere within a
hundred miles of the Erebus and Terror, it is not
likely that those poor fellows would have quitted
their ships in a season so rigorous, and so long
before the Great Fish River would be open for
navigation. We should be the last to say this if
there were a shadow of foundation for further hope,
either to save life or to obtain such records as would
throw more light on the labours and zeal of those
noble ships' companies.

As those men fell in their last sad struggle to

reach home, their prayer must have been that their countrymen might learn how nobly they accomplished the task they had voluntarily undertaken. That prayer has been granted. As long as Britain exists, or our language is spoken, so long will be remembered and related the glorious fate of the crews of the Erebus and Terror, and how nobly they died in the execution of their duty to their Queen and country.

LONDON:
BRADBURY AND EVANS, PRINTERS, WHITEFRIARS.

Made in the USA
Coppell, TX
04 January 2021